TRANSITIONING INTO PRIMARY SCHOOL

Your Passport to Success in Primary School

C.D. Minnis B.Sc., M.Ed.

Copyright © 2017 Carol D. Minnis

All rights reserved. In accordance with U.S. Copyright Act of 1976, the scanning, uploading and electronic sharing of any part of this book without permission of the publisher constitute unlawful piracy and theft of the author's intellectual property. No part of this book may be reproduced in any form by any electronic or mechanical means (including photocopying, recording or information storage and retrieval) without permission in writing from the author or publisher. Thank you for your support of the author's rights.

Published by Richter Publishing LLC www.richterpublishing.com

ISBN:1945812087

ISBN-13:9781945812088

DISCLAIMER

This book is designed to provide information on education only. This information is provided and sold with the knowledge that the publisher and author do not offer any legal or medical advice. In the case of a need for any such expertise, consult with the appropriate professional. This book does not contain all information available on the subject. This book has not been created to be specific to any individual people or organization's situation or needs. Reasonable efforts have been made to make this book as accurate as possible. However, there may be typographical and/or content errors. Therefore, this book should serve only as a general guide. This book contains information that might be dated or erroneous and is intended only to educate and entertain. The author and publisher shall have no liability or responsibility to any person or entity regarding any loss or damage incurred, or alleged to have incurred, directly or indirectly, by the information contained in this book or as a result of anyone acting or failing to act upon the information in this book. You hereby agree never to sue and to hold the author and publisher harmless from any and all claims arising out of the information contained in this book. You hereby agree to be bound by this disclaimer, covenant not to sue and release. You may return this book within the guaranteed time period for a full refund. In the interest of full disclosure, this book contains affiliate links that might pay the author or publisher a commission upon any purchase from the company. While the author and publisher take no responsibility for any virus or technical issues that could be caused by such links, the business practices of these companies and/or the performance of any product or service, the author or publisher has used the product or service and makes a recommendation in good faith based on that experience. All characters appearing in this work have given permission for their photos to be published. Any resemblance to real persons, living or dead, is purely coincidental. The opinions and stories in this book are the views of the author and not that of the publisher.

DEDICATED TO OUR MOTHER
EVELYN GERTRUDE TAYLOR-MINNIS
NOVEMBER 15TH, 1935- NOVEMBER 20TH, 2016

You were the best woman any child could have had for a mother. We were blessed to be raised by you. Your selflessness was remarkable. Not only did you make us, your children, feel loved, but you had a gift of making each person you came into contact with feel special. To know you, was to love you.

Thank you for teaching us how to be respectful, honest, obedient, generous and resilient. More importantly, thank you for teaching us to fear God and walk in His ways.

ACKNOWLEDGEMENTS

Editors: Mrs. Suzanne Knowles – Ministry of Education
Mrs. Dellie Robinson-Thompson – Language Arts Teacher, Government High School
Ms. Joan Norman – Former Language Arts Department Head, St. Anne's School
Mrs. Barbara Petersen – Professional Proofreading Services, New Jersey, USA

Mrs. Bridgewater – Former Principal of Woodcock Primary School

Mrs. Farrington – Former Principal of Sadie Curtis Primary School

Mrs. Sharmaine Forbes – Guidance Counselor, Woodcock Primary School

Nurse Reckell Dillon

Amare Miller – Bahamas Academy Elementary

Noelle Symonette – Sadie Curtis Primary School

Keanell and KeanoTonny – St. Bede's Primary School

Theo Deeron Gibson – St. Cecilia's Primary School

Kenya Wong and Erica Moss – United Estates Primary School, San Salvador

Dexter and Danielle Storr – San Salvador

Ryan Johnson – Briland Bridge Academy, Harbour Island

Benry Jr. and D'Ontre Smith – Fresh Creek Primary School, Andros

Hosea and Ari Hinsey – Love Hill, Andros

Adria and Adrian Hanna – Cleveland Eneas Primary School

Students of Woodcock Primary

Security officers: Mr. Philip Robinson
Ms. Shirley Capron

INTRODUCTION

Primary School is a significant milestone for a five- or six-year-old. Children often feel fearful and anxious about going to a new school and a new environment. There will be many more students, and teachers. Students will take more subjects than when they were in pre-school.

The objective of this book is to help the grade 1 student settle as quickly as possible, so he/she can be about the business of learning. Every school age child in Primary School, in the Commonwealth of The Bahamas, from Inagua in the south to Grand Bahamas in the north, can benefit from using this book.

In the absence of a Guidance Counselor, the student, with the help of the Homeroom teacher, Family Life teacher and parent can still use the materials in this book. The information required will place the counselor or teacher in a better position to assist the student.

From this book, the student will learn:
   a. Ways to help himself/herself successfully survive primary school.
   b. Study skills to perform better in school.
   c. Skills for building self-esteem.
   d. Skills for handling bullies.
   e. The rights of the child/Safe Touches/Unsafe Touches.
   f. How to properly use the internet.
   g. How to manage money at an early age.

These are valuable skills that should be beneficial to the grade 1 student for the rest of his/her life.

Additionally, parents are asked to play an active role in the life of their child by utilizing the tools included in this book. These helpful tools will assist parents in monitoring the progress of their child.

I wish a smooth transition into primary school for every child and parent who uses this book.

C.D. Minnis

7 Reasons the Student Needs This Book:

1. You will **SETTLE** quickly into the rudiments of your new school.

2. You will **CULTIVATE** school spirit for your new school.

3. You will set **EXPECTATIONS** and **GOALS** for yourself, and you will **DETERMINE** how you will achieve them.

4. You will form a closer **BOND** with your parents.

5. You will **UNDERSTAND** and **APPRECIATE** the role of your Guidance Counselor /teacher.

6. You will **GET ALONG** with friends and classmates.

7. You will be a **SUPERSUCCESSFUL** student.

7 Reasons Parents Need This Book:

1. You will be able to monitor the **SUCCESS** of your child's academic performance.

2. You will **PARTNER** with the school to ensure the success of your child.

3. You will be more **AWARE** of challenges your child may be experiencing in school.

4. You will be more **INVOLVED** in the development of your child's physical, mental, spiritual and social life.

5. You will **UNDERSTAND** that your child needs you, as a parent, to be actively involved in his/her life.

6. You will form a **CLOSER BOND** with your child.

7. You will **APPRECIATE** the important role the Guidance Counselor/teacher plays in the life of your child.

7 Reasons the Guidance Counselor/ Teacher Needs This Book:

1. You will be more **SUCCESSFUL** with your students.

2. You will have more **CONTACT** with your students' parents.

3. You will work **CLOSER** with administrators and teachers.

4. You will feel **BETTER** about your role in the life of the students.

5. You will be better **ORGANIZED**.

6. You will feel **LESS STRESSED**.

7. You will be more **RESPECTED** as a professional.

TABLE OF CONTENT

Chapter 1 ……..Welcome to Grade 1 ………………………………….. 11

Chapter 2 …….. Primary School Survival Skills ………………………. 17

Chapter 3 …….. Your Guidance Counselor ………………………………. 21

Chapter 4 …….. Study Skills ……………………………………………... 25

Chapter 5 …….. Building Self-Esteem ……………………………………... 30

Chapter 6 …….. The Rights of the Child/Safe Touches/Unsafe Touches… 36

Chapter 7 …….. Overcoming Bullying ……………………………………..41

Chapter 8 …….. Smart Saver ……………………………………………….45

Chapter 9 …….. Proper Use of the Internet, Social Media & Cell Phones.. 50

Chapter 10 …….Parental Involvement ……………………………………. 54

Appendix A…... Student Progress Report ………………………………….60
Appendix B…... Emergency Contact Numbers ……………………………. 61
Appendix C……School Supplies………………………………………………..62
Appendix D……Student Information Sheet ……………………………….. 63
Appendix E........ Group Counseling Consent Form ……………………….. 65
Appendix F…… Individual Counseling Consent Form …………………….67
Appendix G …...Certificate of Completion…………………………………..69

CHAPTER 1
WELCOME TO GRADE 1

Letter to Parent/Guardian

Dear Parent/Guardian,

We are starting chapter 1 on _____ (Date)
Your child will learn about the importance of wearing proper uniform to school each day. Also, the school's Senior Master or Mistress will speak on the importance of obeying the school's rules. Additionally, a police officer will be invited to speak to the students about rules and laws.

By the end of this chapter, your child should learn the following:
1. Why it is important to keep order in the classroom, the school, the community and in the country.
2. About the school's patron and the administrative team.
3. Your child's daily timetable.
4. What to expect on the Grade Level Assessment Test (GLAT) examinations.

Warmest regards,

_____
Guidance Counselor/Teacher

BONDING ACTIVITY

Together with your child, list five (5) reasons why he/she should attend school in proper uniform every day.

1. _____
2. _____
3. _____
4. _____
5. _____
   _____

2 Corinthians 5:17 - "Therefore, if anyone is in Christ, he is a new creation. The old has passed away; behold, the new has come."

Am I in the right school?
Will I like my new teachers?
Will I get lost on the playground?
Who will be my new buddies?
Will I get to sleep at nap time?
Will I get to play on the playground?

New school. New uniform. New teachers. New friends. You think you are ready. You are not sure if you want to leave your old school and old friends. Your parents have enrolled you in a new school, and you are moving on up from pre-school to primary education.

Description of my new school

The name of my Primary School is _____
My school is named after _____
Telephone number(s) are _____
School colors are _____

Instruction: Students will create a poster outlining the school's rules.

THE ADMINISTRATIVE TEAM- The school is headed by a Principal. There is a Vice-Principal, a Senior Master and a Senior Mistress.

1. My new Principal's name is _____
2. The Vice-Principal's name is _____
3. The Senior Master's name is _____
4. The Senior Mistress' name is _____

HOMEROOM TEACHER - You will have a homeroom teacher who will keep a register. Your homeroom teacher will mark you present each day when you are at school, and absent when you are not at school. Your homeroom teacher will teach most of your subjects.

1. My homeroom teacher's name is _____
2. My homeroom is _____ (e.g. 1T) and, we are in room _____
3. There are _____ students in my homeroom class.

My School's Vision Statement: _____
_____

My School's Mission Statement: _____
_____

The School's Prayer: _____
_____
_____

The School's Pledge: _____
_____

The School's Motto: _____

The Words of the School's Song: _____
_____
_____
_____
_____
_____
_____
_____
_____
_____
_____
_____
_____

You are attending a new school which means new uniform. Describe your school's uniform.

Crest _____
Socks _____
Skirt _____
Pants _____
Necktie _____
Criss-cross tie _____
Blouse _____
Shirt _____
Jumper _____

Paste a picture of you in your new school uniform

Minnis /Primary School / 15

EXERCISE AND TEXTBOOKS - You will need to have a different exercise book for each class. You will get more subjects in primary school. You may have a different teacher for some subjects like Music, Spanish, and Physical Education.

TESTS AND QUIZZES - Your teachers will test you periodically to ensure you understand the lessons. The Grade Level Assessment Test (GLAT) is administered as follows:
   Grade 3: Subjects examined: English Language and Mathematics.
   Grade 6: Subjects examined: English Language, Mathematics, Science and Social Studies.

MINISTRY OF EDUCATION THE COMMONWEALTH OF THE BAHAMAS
BAHAMAS GRADE LEVEL ASSESSMENT TEST STUDENT PROFILE

JADEN NEYMOUR
BEHRING POINT PRIMARY SCHOOL / School Candidate

		GRADE
Mathematics:	Mathematical Concepts	A (a)
Mathematics:	Computation	A (a)
Mathematics:	Application	A (a)
Language Arts:	Writing	A (a)
Language Arts:	Reading Comprehension	A (a)
Language Arts:	Listening Comprehension	A (a)
Language Arts:	Language Skills	A (a)

Printed 29/07/16 at 16:

STUDENT'S TIMETABLE					
	MONDAY	**TUESDAY**	**WEDNESDAY**	**THURSDAY**	**FRIDAY**
PERIOD 1					
PERIOD 2					
PERIOD 3					
PERIOD 4					
PERIOD 5					
PERIOD 6					

BREAK: _____ a.m. - _____ a.m.
LUNCH: _____ p.m. - _____ p.m.

Instruction: To promote school spirit, each student will create a 4-minute Photo Story about his/her new school entitled, *"My school is the best school in The Bahamas."*

SCHOOL NURSE - The nurse is assigned to your school in case you have a medical emergency during the day. The nurse can refer you for further help from a doctor or hospital.

  The name of my school's nurse is:

    1. _____

SECURITY OFFICER(S) – The security officer(s) are stationed at the entrance of your school to check visitors coming on campus to ensure you are safe at all times. Periodically, the security officer(s) will patrol the campus. The names of my school's security officers are:

    1. _____

    2. _____

The support staff will help maintain a clean, green and pristine environment for you to learn and grow in. Name your school's support staff. Our janitors are:

1. _____
2. _____
3. _____
4. _____
5. _____

The yardman is: _____

I acknowledge my child has successfully completed chapter 1.

_____   _____
Parent/Guardian Signature   Date

Chapter 2
Primary School Survival Skills

Letter to Parent/Guardian

Dear Parent/Guardian,
We are starting chapter 2 on _____ (Date).
In this chapter, your child will learn tips on successfully surviving primary school. With these tips, he/she will certainly maximize his/her experiences at his/her new school.

Warmest regards,

_____
Guidance Counselor/Teacher

BONDING ACTIVITY
On a scale of 1-10, have your child rate his/her experience at school. Once he/she has given a rating, have him/her explain how he/she got the rating.

_____
_____
_____
_____
_____
_____

Philippians 4:13 - "I can do everything through Christ who gives me strength."

Your Primary School years can be a fantastic time for you. You will get to meet new people and make new friends. You will learn new subjects. You will go on many field trips. You can earn excellent grades. To achieve these marvelous things will depend on how well you maneuver your way from grades 1 through 6.

Complete the map using the words below:

SMILING, BEING RESPECTFUL, BEING COURTEOUS, FOLLOWING DIRECTIONS, THINKING, WAITING CALMLY/PATIENTLY

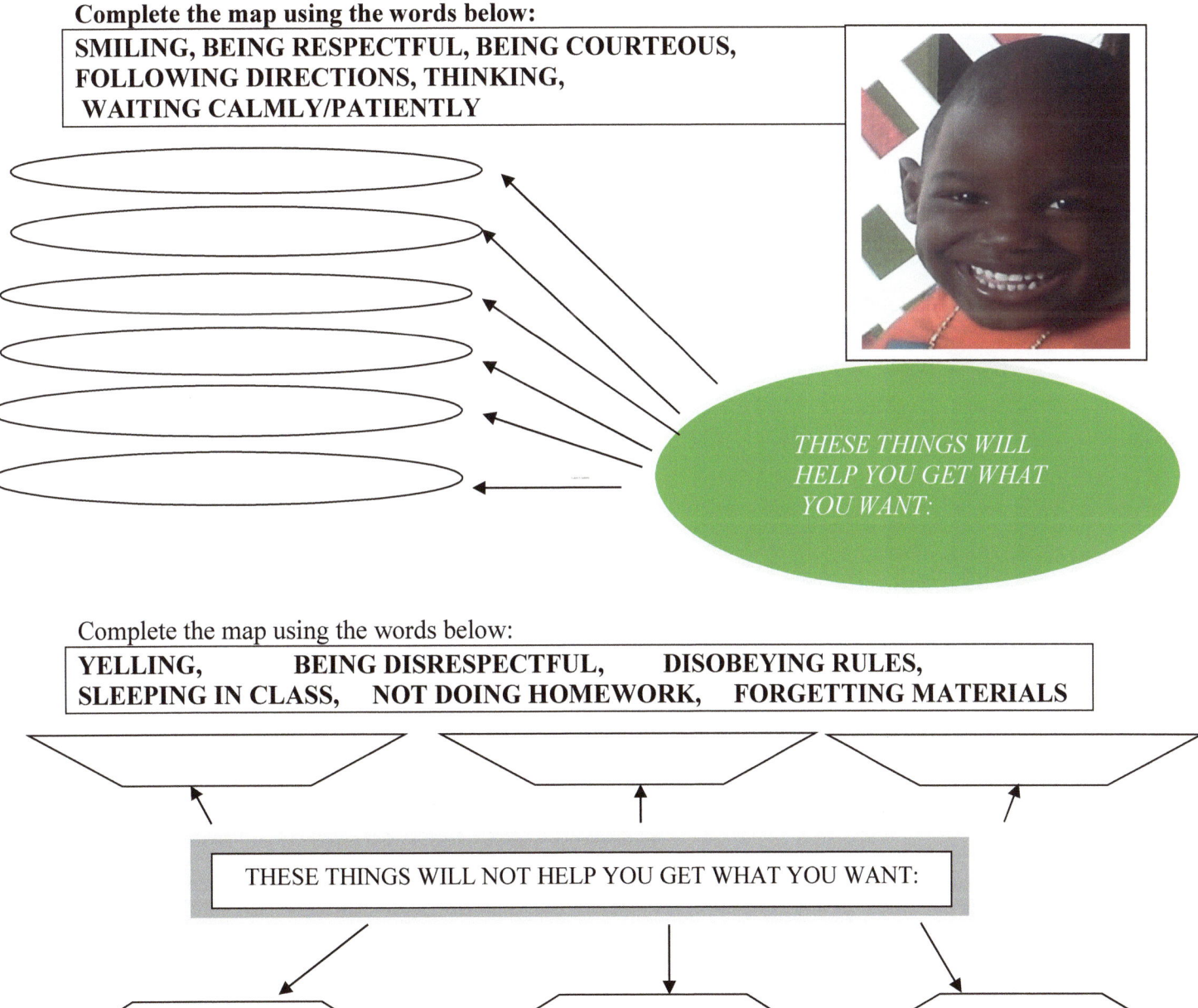

THESE THINGS WILL HELP YOU GET WHAT YOU WANT:

Complete the map using the words below:

YELLING, BEING DISRESPECTFUL, DISOBEYING RULES, SLEEPING IN CLASS, NOT DOING HOMEWORK, FORGETTING MATERIALS

THESE THINGS WILL NOT HELP YOU GET WHAT YOU WANT:

IF TEN THOUSAND PEOPLE DO A FOOLISH THING, IT IS STILL A STUPID THING. -Chinese Proverb

MY PLEDGE

I, _____ (Name)
pledge to use my best manners, to be helpful, to be polite and to be respectful.

I pledge to complete my assignments on time and to have all necessary supplies (books, pencils, eraser, ruler, crayons, etc.).

I pledge to earn excellent grades so that I can be an excellent student.
Date: _____

Dean's Blue Hole – Long Island, Bahamas
"You have unlimited abilities." C.D. Minnis

I acknowledge my child has successfully completed chapter 2.

_____   _____
Parent/Guardian's Signature   Date

Chapter 3
Your Guidance Counselor

Letter to Parent/Guardian

Dear Parent/Guardian,
We are starting chapter 3 on _____ (Date).
In this chapter, you will learn about the role of the Guidance Counselor at your child's school. Your child will understand and appreciate that he/she can always seek the assistance of the counselor for personal/social issues, academic and career planning.

Warmest regards,

_____
Guidance Counselor/Teacher

BONDING ACTIVITY

Assist your child with creating a list of ways he/she can receive assistance from the Guidance Counselor.

_____
_____
_____
_____
_____

Proverbs 1:5 – "Let the wise hear and increase in learning and the one who understands obtain guidance."

Your school may have more than one Guidance Counselor. Your Guidance Counselor will work along with the Administrative team and your teachers to ensure you have a meaningful Primary School experience.

WHEN DO YOU NEED TO SEE YOUR COUNSELOR?
- ❖ Are you anxious about your new school and finding it difficult to adjust?
- ❖ Do you feel overwhelmed by being in a bigger school with more students?
- ❖ Do you feel there are too many subjects for you to learn?

You might be angry, sad, unhappy or find yourself worried all the time. These are all good reasons to visit your Guidance Counselor.

Talk To Your Counselor. Sometimes it is hard to trust other people who are not a member of your family. Your school counselor will help you overcome shyness, resist peer pressure and deal with stress. You are not alone. You can trust your counselor who will be there for you.

Your Counselor Wants To Help You. Your counselor is always available for you. Remember, when you see the counselor, it does NOT mean you are in trouble, or you are crazy. Also, your counselor will check on you to see how you are adjusting to Primary School.

What's On Your Mind?
Are you having trouble in school?
Are you getting along with other students?
Are you being bullied?
Are you worried about something that is happening at home?
Think about what you want to talk about so you can tell your counselor everything and get help.

Be Open and Honest. Benjamin Franklin said, "Honesty is the Best Policy." Always tell the truth even when it may get you in trouble. Being honest will help the counselor solve the problem. However, being open is a little different from being honest. When you are open, it means you are saying what is on your mind. So, you must be open and honest if you want your counselor to help you.

Listen To Your Counselor. Depending on the reason you are visiting your counselor you may get possible solutions to a problem. You and your counselor will brainstorm together and figure out several ideas for solving your problem. Your counselor might have to call your parents to help work out the problem. The solution will only work if you listen to your counselor and then make a commitment to follow through with necessary changes.

You are always welcomed in the counselor's office. So, make an appointment or just drop in to see your counselor today.

I acknowledge my child has successfully completed chapter 3.

_____   _____
     Parent/ Guardian's Signature   Date

Chapter 4
Study Skills

Letter to Parent/Guardian

Dear Parent/Guardian,
We are starting chapter 4 on _____(Date).
In this section, your child will learn how to develop sound study habits. He/she will also learn tips on how to study for examinations. The Primary School Student of the Year will be invited to address students on the topic: *"What it takes to be successful in Primary School."*

Warmest regards,

_____
Guidance Counselor/Teacher

BONDING ACTIVITY
Together with your child, create a workable study timetable he/she will be able to follow each day.

Day	Time	Time	Time	Time
Monday				
Tuesday				
Wednesday				
Thursday				
Friday				
Saturday				
Sunday				

Proverbs 18:15 – "An intelligent heart acquires knowledge, and the ear of the wise seeks knowledge."

"I am a student of Excellence."

"I am a student of excellence.
I studied all the time
I did my homework; I passed all of my tests
I came first
I am on the Honor Roll
I am the Best."

By Amare Miller – Grade 3, Bahamas Academy

The only time success comes before work is in the dictionary. You must always study. Ask questions when you don't understand. Always pay attention. Make studying a habit. Do not put off doing your work for later – do it as planned.

Do not study if you are:
1. Hungry
2. Tired
3. Too cold/hot
4. Too comfortable/uncomfortable
5. Worried or upset
6. Too distracted
7. Sick

Do have the following:

1. Your assignment notebook
2. Solid flat surface for writing
3. Good lighting
4. Chair
5. Books
6. Supplies
7. Computer (Optional)
8. Glasses (wear them if you are supposed to)

Photo courtesy of www.fodors.com

Mount Alvernia, Cat Island, Bahamas

"With perseverance, you can overcome any mountain."

Complete all homework before you begin studying. A study timetable will help you stay focused. It adds structure and is a great habit to have. As you prepare to create your study timetable, look at all the activities you have each day.

E.g., Tuesdays – 3:00 p.m. – 5: 00 p.m.: Band practice
Thursdays – 3:15 p.m. – 4:15 p.m.: Music classes
Saturdays – 9:00 a.m. – 11:00 a.m.: Soccer

TIME	4p.m.-4:30p.m.	5p.m.-5:30p.m.	6p.m.-6:30p.m.
MONDAY		MATHS	
TUESDAY			READING
WEDNESDAY		ENGLISH	
THURSDAY			BIBLE
FRIDAY			

TIME	10a.m.-10:30a.m.	11a.m.-11:30a.m.	12p.m.- 12:30p.m.
SATURDAY			SPANISH
SUNDAY			

TIME	4p.m.-4:30p.m.	5p.m.-5:30p.m.	6p.m.- 6:30p.m.
SATURDAY			
SUNDAY	MUSIC		

What to do before test day?

Instructions: Name each picture. Write words from the box.

| Dress for Success | Eat Breakfast | Make Flash Cards |
| Study with a buddy | Take the supplies you need | Don't cram |

1. _____

2. _____

3. _____

4. _____

5. _____

6. _____

Have a goal in mind. You are working to receive excellent grades. Your rewards will be great as long as you work hard.

I acknowledge my child has successfully completed chapter 4.

_____   _____

Parent/Guardian's Signature   Date

Chapter 5
Building Self-Esteem

Letter to Parent/Guardian

Dear Parent/Guardian,
We are starting chapter 5 on _____ (Date).
In this chapter, we will learn how your child can develop a high self-esteem. He/she will understand that he/she is a remarkable individual who has the potential to become a great human being with the ability to contribute positively to society.

Warmest regards,

_____
Guidance Counselor/Teacher

BONDING ACTIVITY
Assist your child with creating a poem entitled, "*Me.*"

_____
_____
_____
_____
_____
_____
_____
_____
_____
_____
_____

Psalm 139:14 - "I Praise You Because I Am Fearfully and Wonderfully Made."

Your self-esteem has to do with how you feel about yourself. How you feel about yourself may be influenced by your parents, sisters and brothers, and your friends. Only you can decide how much you want others to control how you feel about yourself.

People with high self-esteem work hard to improve their weak areas so that those areas can become strong. They also work hard to keep their strong areas high. Some characteristics of high self-esteem are:

1. Confidence
2. Self-driven/motivated
3. Forgiving
4. Problem solver
5. Trusting

People with low self-esteem are always worrying about what others say about them, or how others treat them. They care more about the opinion of other people than they care about their opinion. They feel negative about themselves. Some characteristics of low self-esteem are:

1. Negative
2. Perfectionist
3. Mistrusting
4. Dependent
5. Fearful
6. Doubting

Ways to build your Self-Esteem:
1. Be fair with yourself. You are not perfect.
2. Be positive.
3. Have a helpful attitude.
4. Practice taking care of yourself.
5. Know your strengths and weaknesses.
6. Stay away from people who don't have good things to say about you.
7. Stay around people who have good things to say and who always encourage you.
8. Be respectful when telling others how you feel.

Instructions: Trace a picture of your hand in the space below. Write a positive attribute about yourself for each finger.

SELF-ESTEEM WORD PUZZLE

Find the following hidden words:

    confident, respect, positive, praise, strong, happy, trust,
    caring, loving, smart, friendly, excellent, beautiful, handsome, likable

```
J E L S M O I C V N A E J Y S G A D V Q
T W H R L A P A T S Y L E I R X E O V O
M E E L W E N R T L E E S X I H N R O S
D H S J I S A I D O D L V S W Q W S I E
Y M T X P K Y N P V A P L F G J S E N P
K E R C V T E G D I V B W C N M F R Z S
I A U O S I W A S N C I E D D E O A S N
Q G S N R C P O B G I R A L A E M E E G
E I T F H W O E T L O B U L G S S N J K
O X N I Y R S Y E R E F E S G N E M S F
N H C D B L I M S I I O I E K U M T S A
O A A E F I T O A T P T S Z S R E D N V
G H R N L V I I U R B R T T P E A O O O
W A K T D L V A G G T I C H I E W I N U
E P R A I S E N I D C E E T L E D N U O
Y P R E D B O N F P P O J M G T C T L F
V Y F I E R G M T S E B B L S P E V T G
H T R E T E T E E F M C N R O U P N O B
T R Q S S S Y R C N A L F A M I A Y X C
M Y O N M I Z N E T M S O H W W D E H N
```

AFFIRM YOURSELF DAILY

    "I AM A POSITIVE PERSON"   "I AM TALENTED"

    "I LOVE MYSELF"   "I AM BEAUTIFUL"

        "I AM AWESOME"

Instruction:
A. Create a collage of yourself using pictures from baby to present. OR
B. Draw a picture of you doing your favorite activity (e.g., playing a basketball game, video games, baking, etc.)

House of Assembly – Nassau, Bahamas
"You can make a difference." C.D. Minnis

LIVING THE BAHAMIAN DREAM

It is always important to dream. But, as you dream and plan your future, always remember to be faithful to God, country, family and yourself.

Your school, the first computer, the first airplane, the first mall were built because someone had a dream.

What do you dream of achieving in life? Create your "Bahamian Dream."

Instructions:
1. Make a list of all the things you want in life (good grades, career, tablet, clothes, car, home, vacations, etc.)
2. Collect pictures of these items (look in magazines, computer)
3. Get a large poster board (Your favorite color)
4. Paste the photos on the board
5. Mount your dream board where you can see it every day to keep you motivated.

I acknowledge my child has successfully completed chapter 5.

_____   _____

Parent/Guardian's Signature   Date

Chapter 6
The Rights of the Child
Safe Touches/Unsafe Touches

Letter to Parent/Guardian

Dear Parent/Guardian,
We are starting chapter 6 on _____(Date).
In this chapter, your child will learn how to identify different types of touches. Your child will understand it is okay to let others know when he/she feels as though his/her personal space has been invaded.

Warmest regards,

_____
Guidance Counselor/Teacher

BONDING ACTIVITY
List ways you can tell someone not to invade your personal space.
1. _____
2. _____
3. _____
4. _____
5. _____
6. _____
7. _____
8. _____

1 Corinthians 3:16 – "Do you not know that you are God's temple and that God's Spirit dwells in you?"

The Child Protection Act, published January 16, 2007, in the Gazette of The Bahamas, outlines the following as guiding principles in the protection of the child:
1. Rights of the Child
2. Legal Capacity and Guardianship of Children
3. Custody
4. Family maintenance, maintenance rights and duties of members of the family as between themselves
5. Proceedings to enforce right to maintenance
6. Care and protection of children supervision orders
7. Approved children homes
8. Establishment, functions, and terms of reference of the national committee for families and children
9. Proceedings involving children
10. Representation and monitoring of Children's Registry
11. Children detained or brought before a court
12. Juvenile courts
13. Places of detention
14. Miscellaneous

> **Directions: In groups of 4, students will create a poster on four (4) different unalienable rights of the child. One student from each group will present their group's work to the class.**

Child Protection Month is April of each year. The Bahamas, like many countries around the world, uses the pinwheel as a symbol of child abuse prevention.

The adage, "it takes a village to raise a child" can still make a difference in the life of a child. Children need to feel loved in the home, church, school, and certainly in their neighborhood. Unfortunately, this is not always the case, and young, innocent children are sometimes taken advantage of.

Too often children find themselves abused physically, verbally, emotionally and sexually. Also, many children suffer from neglect by the adults in their lives. Social Services Department reported there are 400 – 600 cases of abuse each year, with a lot of cases going unreported.

2012 - 636 cases,   2013 - 490 cases,   2014 - 597 cases

Sadly, children are betrayed by those persons who are in a position to protect them. Sometimes these individuals are a parent, relative or friend of the family. These abused and neglected children are told:
1. "You will get into trouble if you tell anyone."
2. "No one is going to believe you."
3. "We will take away your privileges."
4. "You made me do that to you."

Children need to remember that "abuse is not their fault, they are the victim."

Identify your feelings. Write the correct feelings in each column.

FEELING WORDS: SAD, ANGRY, JOVIAL, CALM, THOUGHTFUL, NERVOUS, SCARED, JOYFUL, HAPPY, APPREHENSIVE

BAD FEELING WORDS	GOOD FEELING WORDS
1. ------------------------------------	1. ------------------------------------
2. ------------------------------------	2. ------------------------------------
3. ------------------------------------	3. ------------------------------------
4. ------------------------------------	4. ------------------------------------
5. ------------------------------------	5. ------------------------------------

ABUSE - Beating, Slapping, Insulting, Controlling, Pushing, Isolating, Threatening, Putting down, Withholding.

According to the Crisis Center of The Bahamas, some of the signs of sexual abuse are as follows:
- Precocious sexual behavior
- Unexplained bleeding or discharge from genital or anal areas
- Stress-related disorders
- Infections in the mouth or throat
- Sexually transmitted diseases
- Loss of appetite
- Unexplained vomiting or gagging
- Nightmares
- Anxiety
- Withdrawal
- Low self-esteem
- Problems at school

Name five fundraising initiatives that assist abused and neglected children.

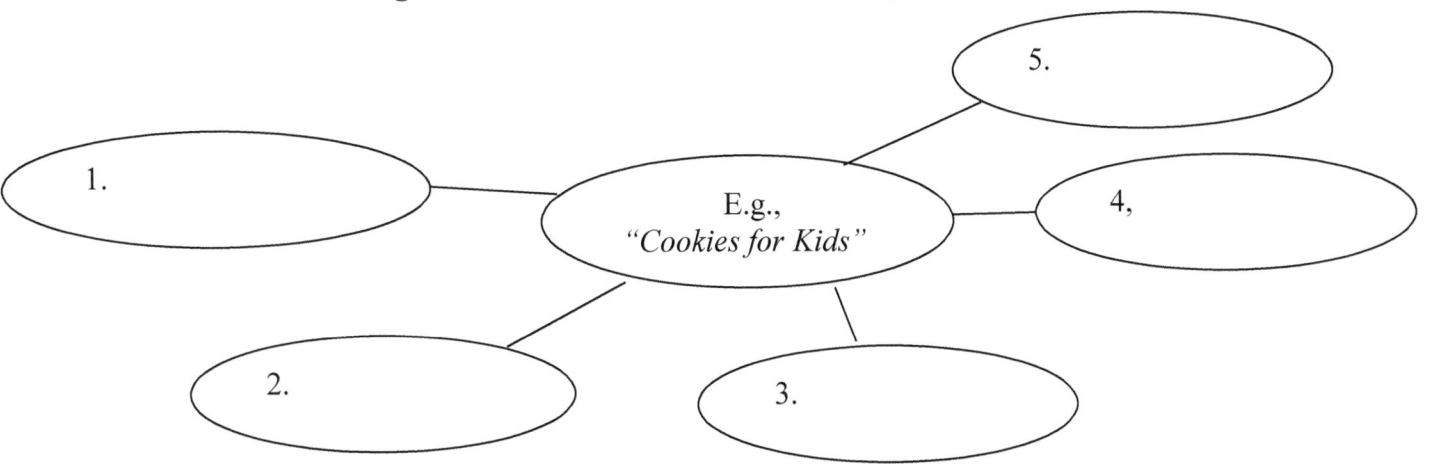

Neglected or sexually, physically, verbally or emotionally abused children should ask anyone of these persons for help:

Family members- Mother, Father, Siblings	Godparents
Aunts, Uncles, Grandparents	Guidance Counselor
Sunday School Teacher	Neighbor
Teacher	Police/Urban Renewal

Instructions: Complete the list of agencies that will assist a child when it is suspected the child is being abused or neglected.

1. The National Child Protection Council
2. The Department of Social Services & Community Development
3. The Suspected Child Abuse & Neglect (SCAN)
4. Unit of the Department of Public Health, Ministry of Health
5. _____
6. _____

St. Stephen's Anglican Church November 2009 – Fresh Creek, Andros
"Jesus can help you through it all." C.D. Minnis
(This church was destroyed by fire May 2010)

I acknowledge my child has successfully completed chapter 6.

_____   _____
Parent/Guardian's Signature   Date

Chapter 7
Overcoming Bullying

Letter to Parent/Guardian

Dear Parent/Guardian,
We are starting chapter 7 on _____(Date).
A guest speaker will present on the effects of bullying. By the end of this section, your child will learn coping skills if he/she is being bullied. We will also learn tips on how your child should not be a bully with peers.

Warmest regards,

_____
Guidance Counselor/Teacher

BONDING ACTIVITY
Assist your child with making a poster that depicts how someone would feel who is being bullied.

James 1:19 - "...be quick to listen, slow to speak, and slow to anger."
John 15:12 - "This is my commandment, that you love one another as I have loved you."

> "People who have had drama and pain,
> want others to feel that pain."
> Rudolph Brutus
> Grade 6
> Claridge Primary School

WHAT IS BULLYING?

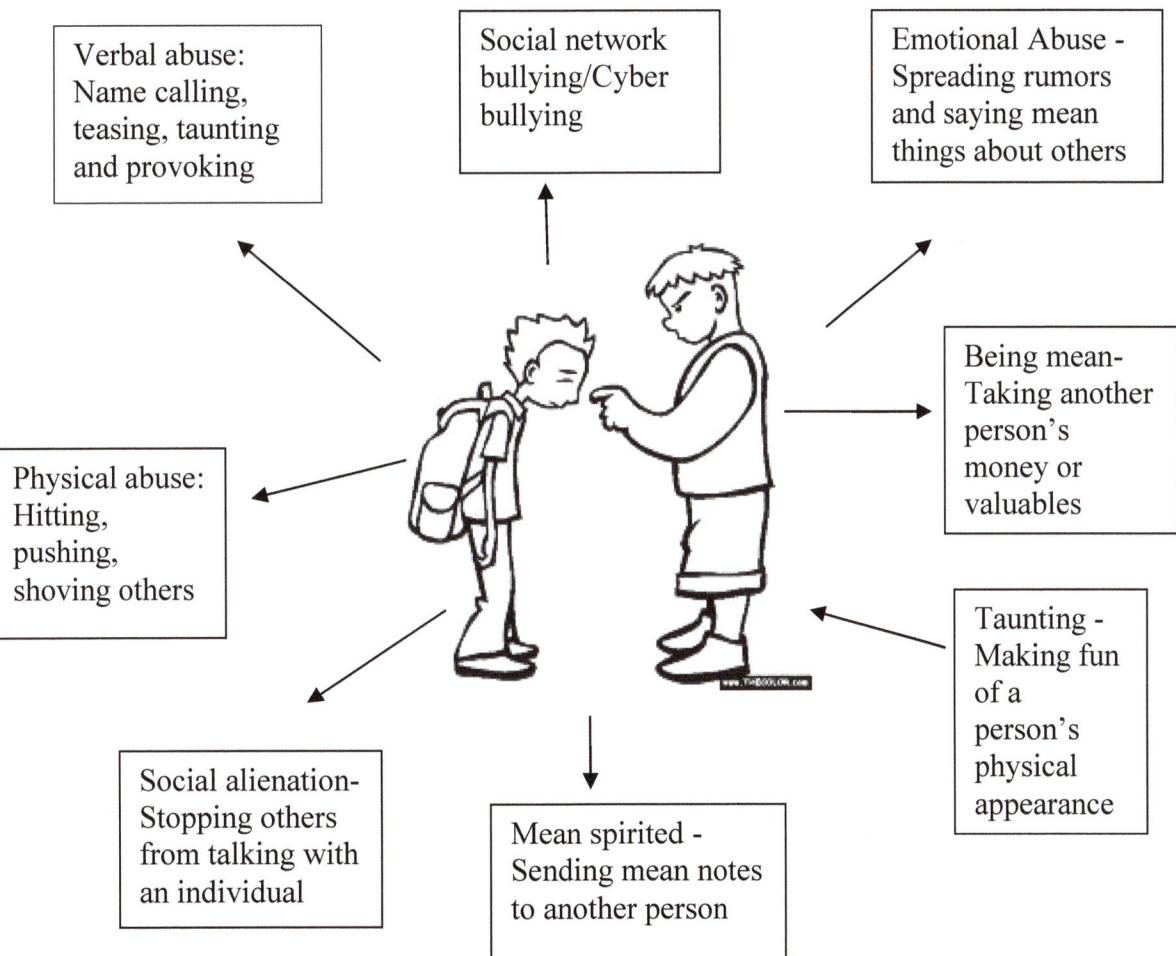

Adapted from www.Mumsnet – By Parents for Parents.com

According to the *"Bahamas Secondary School Drug Prevalence Survey 2012"* conducted by National Anti-Drug Secretariat of The Bahamas National Drug Council, it was discovered that male and female students are both likely to be bullied by their peers. Also, male and female students exhibit aggressive behaviors when bullying others.

Minnis/ Primary School / 44

Instruction: Students, while working in pairs, will list unacceptable and acceptable behaviors when interacting with peers.

How does bullying make you feel?

ALONE   NERVOUS   LONELY   ANGRY

WORRIED   MAD   SCARED

Bullying makes me feel _____

What do you do when you are bullied? Tell someone. Tell your Guidance Counselor, your parents, a teacher or a sibling.

What to do if you are the bully? What if you are the one bullying? Bullying is not a good behavior. You are hurting others. Your behavior is not good. You are not being a good person. Say sorry to the person you are bullying, and don't do it again.

Stop it now! It hurts others, and it is wrong!

I acknowledge my child has successfully completed chapter 7.

_____   _____

Parent/Guardian's Signature   Date

Chapter 8
Smart Saver

Letter to Parent/Guardian

Dear Parent/Guardian,
We are starting chapter 8 on _____ (Date).
In this section, we will learn why it is the importance to save. Additionally, by the end of this section, your child will learn about being involved in a civic organization and giving of his/her time and talent to assist other individuals. Students will visit an organization on a field trip. The following guest speakers will be invited:
1. Someone from a civic organization to speak on, *"Helping the less fortunate in your Community."*
2. A representative from a bank or credit union who will give students tips on how to save.

Warmest regards,

_____
Guidance Counselor/Teacher

BONDING ACTIVITY
Assist your child with developing good saving habits by each of you saving a dollar a day.

Proverbs 13:11-"Wealth gained hastily will dwindle, but whoever gathers little by little will increase it."

YOU ARE NEVER TOO YOUNG TO SAVE

Children need to learn about money at an early age. Knowing about money includes saving, spending, donating and investing. Commonwealth Bank has a *Kids Savings Club and a Christmas Account.* Bank of The Bahamas encourages young people to open *a Junior Account* with as little as $20. First Caribbean International Bank offers the *Sure Start* to children. Fidelity Bank invites people to start *Asue* accounts with them. Credit Unions are also another option for saving. Children should be taught to sacrifice to get what they want. They will then fully appreciate the toy or video game they helped to purchase with monies they saved.

According to the January – June 2016 edition of *"The Bahamas Investor,"* "There is a terribly low household savings rate in The Bahamas."

When you have saved some money in your piggy bank, ask you mummy, daddy, godparent, older brother or older sister to take you to the bank so that you can open a bank account.

Instructions: Students will practice filling out deposit slips and balancing saving accounts.

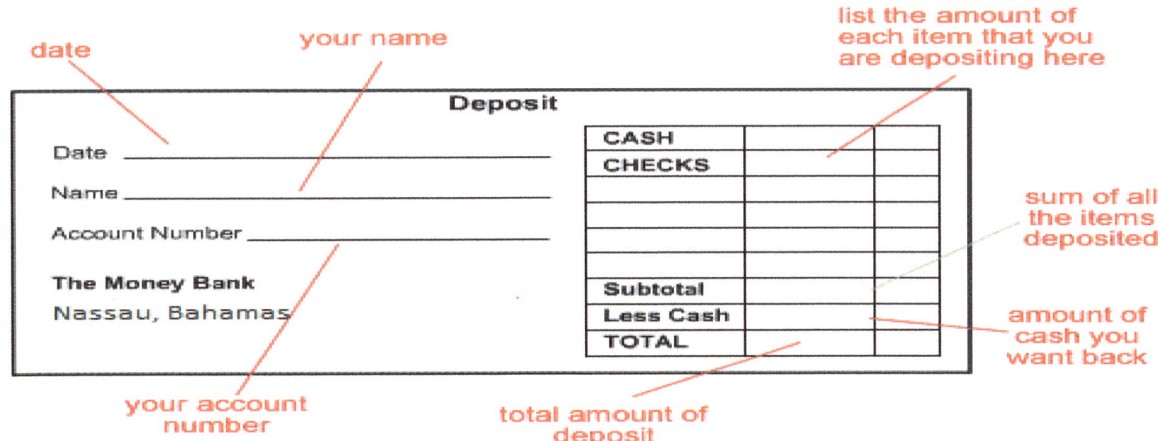

Minnis/ Primary School / 48

YOU CAN SAVE MORE

$1.00 a day for 365 days = a WHOPPING $365.00 in one year.

20__	January	February	March	April	May	June	July	August	September	October	November	December
1												
2												
3												
4												
5												
6												
7												
8												
9												
10												
11												
12												
13												
14												
15												
16												
17												
18												
19												
20												
21												
22												
23												
24												
25												
26												
27												
28												
29												
30												
31												
Total												

"It is more blessed to give than receive." Acts 20:35. It is okay to:
- ✓ Give to others.
- ✓ Donate to charity.
- ✓ Share your lunch with your classmate who doesn't have any.
- ✓ Give the less fortunate boy the extra pair of tennis shoes that have gotten too small for you.

Give your time, talent and treasure for the benefit of others.

TIME TALENT TREASURE

Photo courtesy of Shanta Brown

How do you use your time, talent and treasure? You can use them to:
- Volunteer and help the less fortunate.
- Become a Cub Scout.
- Join Brownies or Sunflowers.

Get involved. Children who are members of clubs and organizations are better socialized. As a member of a club or organization, you give of your time by attending the meetings and events planned by the club. You give of your talent by helping to sell goods or decorating or even writing something for the club. You give of your treasure by donating your money to the club when paying dues or helping with a fundraising event.

> **Instructions: Students will research local civic organizations. They will think of a fund-raising exercise (e.g., make and sell friendship bracelets) and donate the funds to an organization. Students will select an organization where they can perform volunteer work.**

I acknowledge my child has completed chapter 8.

_____   _____

Parent/Guardian's Signature   Date

Chapter 9
Proper use of the Internet, Social Media and Cell Phones

Letter to Parent/Guardian

Dear Parent/Guardian,
We are starting chapter 9 on _____ (Date).
The internet is an awesome tool if used correctly. In this section, your child will learn how to properly use the internet so he/she can maximize his/her potentials. A guest speaker will be invited to address students on how the computer can make a positive difference, or have a devastating impact on his/her life.

Warmest regards,

_____
Guidance Counselor/Teacher

BONDING ACTIVITY
Together with your child, create a list of rules for the use of the internet.
1. _____
2. _____
3. _____
4. _____
5. _____
6. _____

Proverbs 4:7 "Getting wisdom is the wisest thing you can do! And whatever else you do, develop good judgment."

POSITIVE USE OF THE INTERNET

You can use the internet in many positive ways.
- To research school work.
- To type and save your work.
- To spell-check and grammar check your work.
- To copy and paste pictures off the internet into your schoolwork to make your work look better.
- To download educational apps to help with homework and classwork.
- You can use the internet to assist you with your school projects.

Directions: Place students in groups of five (5). A fun and easy way to separate students into groups are to use Skittles, M & M's or colored rubber bands. Students will be grouped based on the color he/she selected. Each team will choose one form of technology and show how their chosen technology can be used in the classroom.
(Examples of technology to choose from iPhone, iPod, game devices, Kindle, iPad/tablet, smartphone, MP3 player, computer, etc.)

One of the negative ways you can use the internet is to cyberbully. If you are bullied on the web, keep the threatening messages, pictures and texts so that you can show them to your parents, school or even the police. If you are in the same class with the person who is cyberbullying you, tell your Guidance Counselor so something can be done right away to stop the bullying peacefully.

Adapted from "Cyberbullying: New problems, new tactics." www.kidshealth.org

If you are doing the cyberbullying, then you need to stop this negative behavior. This action might seem harmless, but can hurt feelings and lead to grave consequences at home, school and in the community.

Instructions: Write useful ways of using the computer, cell phone and the iPad, tablet.

COMPUTER	CELL PHONE	iPAD/TABLET

The Original PlayStation, Computer, Wii, cell phone and tablet.

I acknowledge my child has successfully completed chapter 9.

_____   _____

Parent/Guardian's Signature   Date

Chapter 10
Parental Involvement

Letter to Parent/Guardian

Dear Parent/Guardian,

We are starting chapter 10 on _____ (Date). This chapter seeks to encourage you to become fully involved in the success of your child. This section will focus on how you should monitor your child's use of the internet and keeping your child safe online. Additionally, you will be given tips on how you can foster a better relationship with your child.

Warmest regards,

_____
Guidance Counselor/Teacher

BONDING ACTIVITY

You and your child create a list of activities you can do together to foster a better relationship.

_____

_____

_____

_____

_____

Proverbs 22:6 – "Train up a child in the way he should go; even when he is old he will not depart from it."

PARENTAL INVOLVEMENT

Your child needs your help transitioning into Primary School. Your child has been in the same kindergarten school with the same friends for at least two years. This transitional period could be a most difficult time, but with your help, parents, this could happen quickly and without incident.

TIPS FOR PARENTS

1. Spend quality time with your child – take your child to the mall, the beach, the movies.
2. Know the administrators, the guidance counselor, and teachers – get email addresses and phone contacts.
3. Know your child's friends – get the name of parents and phone contacts.
4. Check your child's books – go over classwork and homework.
5. Attend and participate in Parents Teachers Association (P.T.A.) Meetings.
6. Encourage your child to share with you. Assure your child he/she will not get in trouble for sharing what is happening in his/her life.
7. Encourage your child to follow the rules of the school and society.
8. Get a tutor if your child is experiencing difficulties in any subject.
9. Dorothy Law Nolte says, *"Children learn what they live."* Be a living example for your child to emulate.
10. Spend quality time with your child – cook/bake together, play games with your child.

MONITOR YOUR CHILD'S USE OF THE INTERNET:

Inform your child that you will be monitoring his/her use of the web often. Tell your child there will be no privacy when it comes to the internet. Your child must give you every password he/she uses, or you will create one for him/her for all his/her internet accounts.

1. Password protect your home computer, so you can monitor the amount of time your child spends on the web – Do not use passwords like:
   a. your date of birth
   b. your mother's name
   c. your middle name
2. When creating a password, try to mix letters with numbers and symbols. Mixing letters with numbers and symbols make it very challenging for your child to figure out your password.
3. Check your computer's internet history regularly to see which sites your child has been visiting and if they're instant messaging.
4. Let your child know you're monitoring his/her email and messaging accounts to see who he/she is communicating with.
5. Your child will argue at first, but will soon understand and, it should help to prevent accusations of snooping later on.

Talk to your children about the possible dangers of chatting with strangers online and protecting private information - name, phone number, even what school they go to - and never sharing their password information with friends.

Parents, always keep the computer in the family room so that you can monitor their use of the computer. Never allow your child to have a computer in his/her room. Limit the amount of time they spend on the computer. Assign screen time for your child – example T.V. only on weekends, the computer only on weekends, unless it is a school assignment.

KEEP YOUR CHILD … SAFE ONLINE

HANDS-ON PARENTAL INVOLVEMENT
1. Show your child love – give him/her hugs and kisses regularly.
2. Always listen to him/her, even when it seems like he/she is not making any sense. Try to reassure him/her at all times.
3. Speak positively into his/her spirit.
4. Show your child love - Encourage him/her to have an "I can do it" attitude.
5. Assure him/her you are his/her number one fan and will always be there for him/her.
6. Show your child love – show interest in his/her world without judging.

This transitional period is a crucial time in the life of your child. He/she is adjusting to a new environment, new teachers and new friends. A child with peace of mind functions better and reaches his/her potential easier than a child who is always worrying.

Parenting is a twenty-four-hour job. Take advantage of each opportunity you get to do more for your child. By doing this, you will have a better home, we will have a better society, and all of us will make The Bahamas the best little country in the world.

PARENT'S PLEDGE

1. I will **HELP** my child to graduate as an Honor Roll student.
2. I will **TEACH** my child to be respectful to administrators, staff and fellow students.
3. I will **INSTRUCT** my child to obey the school's rules.
4. I will **GUARANTEE** my child attends school in proper uniform each day.
5. I will **ENSURE** my child has all the necessary materials for each class every day.
6. I will **ENCOURAGE** my child to have a positive attitude.
7. I will **FOSTER** an "I can" attitude in my child.
8. I will **TEACH** my child how to say, *"please," "thank you," "pardon me," "excuse me," "may I," "yes sir," "no sir," "yes ma'am," "no ma'am,"* etc.
9. I will **ENSURE** my child comes to school in good health each day.
10. I will **PRAISE** my child when he/she does well and **ENCOURAGE** him/her when he/she is feeling challenged.

WHAT I LEARNED …

Congratulations! I commend you for completing *Transitioning into Primary School.* You are now equipped with skills that will help you develop into a well-rounded individual. You will succeed. You will be an 'A' student at your new school. Use the space below to write one thought that you will remember about each chapter of the book, and how it can help you develop into the successful person you are capable of becoming.

Chapter 1 ……..Welcome to Grade 1 _____

_____

Chapter 2 …….. Primary School Survival Skills _____

_____

Chapter 3 …….. Your Guidance Counselor _____

_____

Chapter 4 …….. Study Skills _____

_____

Chapter 5 …….. Building Self-Esteem _____

_____

Chapter 6 …….. The Rights of the Child/Good Touch/Bad Touch _____

_____

Chapter 7 …….. Overcoming Bullying _____

_____

Chapter 8 …….. Smart Saver _____

_____

Chapter 9 …….. Proper Use of the Internet, Social Media & Cell Phones_____

_____

Chapter 10 …….Parental Involvement _____

_____

APPENDIX A
STUDENT PROGRESS REPORT

SCHOOL: _____ **DATE:** _____

STUDENT: _____ **GRADE:** _____

Your child is a capable student who has lots of ability. To ensure your child realizes his/her full potential, have your child's teachers complete this form, and return it to you so you can monitor your child's progress in school. Have this Student Progress Report form completed once monthly.

SUBJECTS	GRADES TO DATE	TEACHER	COMMENTS	TEACHER'S SIGNATURE
English Language				
Comprehension				
Reading				
Mathematics				
Science				
Religion				
Music				
Spanish				
Physical Education				
Other				

	PLEASE SELECT THE APPROPRIATE COMMENT(S):			
1	Student worked well	9	Excessive talking
2	Student was punctual	10	Student was disruptive
3	Student behaved well	11	Student is tardy
4	Behavior is improving	12	Disrespectful
5	Has all school supplies	13	Refuses to cooperate
6	Completes assignments	14	Needs continual guidance
7	Cooperative, helpful, respectful	15	Parent Conference needed
8	Student has made tremendous improvement		

APPENDIX B
EMERGENCY CONTACT NUMBERS

CALL ANY ONE OF THE FOLLOWING AGENCIES FOR HELP:

AGENCIES	PHONE	PHONE	PHONE
ADOLESCENT HEALTH SERVICES	328-3248/9		
AIDS SECRETARIAT	328-2260	323-5968	325-2281
ALCOHOLIC ANONYMOUS	322-1685		
BAHAMAS NATIONAL DRUG COUNCIL	325-4633/4	326-5355	326-5340
CHILD ABUSE HOTLINE (GRAND BAHAMA)	351-7763		
CHILD ABUSE HOTLINE (NEW PROVIDENCE)	322-2763	422-2763	
CHILD PROTECTION SERVICES	397-2550		
CHRISTIAN COUNSELING CENTER	323-7000		
COMMUNITY COUNSELING & ASSESSMENT CENTER	323-3293		
COMMUNITY MENTAL HEALTH	323-3295/9		
CRIMINAL INVESTIGATION UNIT	322-2561	322-2562	
CRISIS CENTER (GRAND BAHAMA)	352-4357		
CRISIS CENTER (NEW PROVIDENCE)	328-0922	322-4999	
DEPARTMENT OF SOCIAL SERVICES	397-2524		
DOMESTIC VIOLENCE	323-0171	323-3859	
DRUG ENFORCEMENT UNIT	323-7139	323-7140	
HEALTH SOCIAL SERVICES – FAMILY VIOLENCE	356-3350	356-4468	
NATIONAL HOTLINE	322-2763		422-2763
NATIONAL LEAD INSTITUTE	328-5323	525-3749	698-6384
PACE SCHOOL	356-0943		
POLICE	911	919	
POLICE VICTIM SUPPORT	328-5670		
PUBLIC HEALTH DEPARTMENT	502-4700	322-8835	
SANDILANDS REHABILITATION CENTER	364-9600		
SCHOOL PSYCHOLOGICAL SERVICES	502-2948		
SURE	341-2949		
SUSPECTED CHILD ABUSE AND NEGLECT UNIT (SCAN)	322-5823	323-8438	
T.A.P.S.	393-0706	393-0672	394-3064
TEEN CHALLENGE	341-0829		

APPENDIX C

Grade 1

- Pencil box
- Crayons
- Colored pencils
- Washable markers
- No. 2 pencils
- Ballpoint pens
- Pencil sharpener
- Erasers
- Glue sticks
- Ruler
- Blunt-tipped scissors
- Folders
- Assorted construction paper
- Black & White notebook and folder paper
- Tissues
- Hand sanitizer
- Backpack
- Lunchbox or bag
- P.E. Kit
- Textbooks required by the school

APPENDIX D
STUDENT INFORMATION SHEET

Your Guidance Counselor is here to assist you. Please complete this form and return it to your counselor at the beginning of the term.

NAME OF STUDENT: _____

DATE OF BIRTH: _____

PRESCHOOL: _____

HOMEROOM CLASS: _____ HOMEROOM TEACHER: _____

MOTHER'S NAME: _____

PHONE (H)_____ (C)_____ (W)_____

FATHER'S NAME: _____

PHONE (H)_____ (C)_____ (W)_____

STUDENT LIVES WITH: _____

PHONE (H)_____ (C)_____ (W)_____

PHOTO

Do you have any medical/emotional problems that have been medically diagnosed and may affect you during the course of the day? E.g., Asthma, depression, heart condition: ☐ YES ☐ NO

If yes, please list medical/emotional problems: _____

Medication(s) being used: _____

Do you have any known allergies? ☐ YES ☐ NO

If yes, please list allergies: _____

Medication(s) being used: _____

YOUR INTEREST/TALENT

Please place a tick next to the item(s) you are good at:

Artist: ☐ painting ☐ drawing ☐ craft
Agriculture: ☐ growing things (fruits & vegetables and/or flowers)
Athlete: ☐ track and field ☐ basketball ☐ soccer ☐ swimming ☐ volleyball Other _____
☐ Building things from wood
☐ Cooking ☐ baking
Computer: ☐ creating videos ☐ playing games ☐ graphics Other: _____
Electronics: ☐ repairing clocks, television, computers, etc.
Music: ☐ play an instrument ☐ sing ☐ dance Other: _____
Any other interest/talent _____

Minnis/ Primary School / 64

APPENDIX E
Parent/Guardian Consent Form
for Group Counseling

I give permission for my child, _____ of grade _____ to participate in Group Counseling activities.

The Group Counseling will run from _____ to _____.

Some of the subjects to be covered in the group are as follows:

_____

_____

This group will be led by (Ms., Mrs., Mr.) _____ of the Guidance Department.

The group leader(s) will keep the information shared by group members confidential, except in situations where:

1. Any student reveals information about harm to himself/herself or any other person.
2. Any student discloses information about abuse or molestation.
3. Any student divulges information about criminal activity, or the court (a judge) subpoenas counseling records.

The counselor is mandated to report this information to the relevant authority.

By signing this form, I give my informed consent for my child to participate in Group Counseling.

Please print parent/guardian's name _____

Signature of parent/guardian _____

Please print student's name _____

Signature of student _____

Date _____

Minnis/ Primary School / 66

APPENDIX F
Parent/Guardian Consent Form
for Individual Counseling

I give permission for the Guidance Counselor, (Ms., Mrs., Mr.) _____ to conduct Individual Counseling with my child, _____ of grade _____.

The Individual Counseling sessions will run from _____ to _____.

The relationship between counselor and client relies on trust. The counselor will keep the information shared by the student confidential, except in situations where:

1. The student reveals information about harm to himself/herself or any other person.
2. The student discloses information about abuse or molestation.
3. The student divulges information about criminal activity, or the court (a judge) subpoenas counseling records.

The counselor is mandated to report the information immediately to the relevant authority.

By signing this form, I give my informed consent for my child to participate in Individual Counseling.

Please print parent/guardian's name _____

Signature of parent/guardian _____

Please print student's name _____

Signature of student _____

Date _____

APPENDIX G
CERTIFICATE OF COMPLETION

School _____

CERTIFICATE OF COMPLETION

This certificate is awarded to

_____

Congratulations! You have successfully completed *Transitioning Into Primary School.*

_____ _____
Guidance Counselor/Teacher   *Parent/Guardian*

Date: _____

Minnis/ Primary School / 70

REFERENCES

Bahamas Secondary School Drug Prevalence Survey 2012 by National Anti-Drug Secretariat,
    The Bahamas National Drug Council
Positive Classroom Management by Terri Breeden & Emalie Egan
The Parent Institute
Stress, Hope Heart Institute, 1988
The Champion's Ride by Allison Manswell
Photos: Shanta Brown
www.fodor.com
www.Mumsnet – by Parents for Parents.com
The Bahamas Investor January – June 2016 edition

MEET THE AUTHOR

C. D. Minnis worked as a classroom teacher for fifteen (15) years and as a Guidance Counselor for fourteen (14) years. She started her teaching career at Hawksbill High School in Grand Bahama, then moved to Central Andros High School, her alma mater. She later served at L.W. Young Junior/Senior High School, Doris Johnson Senior High School, C.V. Bethel Senior High School, C. I. Gibson Senior High School and is currently posted at the Transitional Alternative Program for Students (T.A.P.S.). Ms. Minnis has interacted with students from all strata of society.

Ms. Minnis completed her graduate studies at Kent State University in collaboration with the now, University of The Bahamas, obtaining a Master of Education in School Counseling. Her Bachelor of Science degree is in Secondary Education from Fort Valley State University, Fort Valley, Georgia. She obtained her high school education at Central Andros High School, Andros, Bahamas.

Ms. Minnis is presently serving as a Guidance Counselor and is employed by the Ministry of Education. As department head and grade level counselor, she worked tirelessly implementing programs to help students realize their full potential. She enjoys working with teenagers and gets much joy out of helping them become responsible and productive citizens.

She is a member of Holy Cross Anglican Church where she serves as an usher. Her favorite scripture verses are Romans 8:28, *"For all things work together for good to those who love The Lord, for those who are called according to His purpose."* Ephesians 3:20 *"Now unto Him, that can do **exceedingly, abundantly above all that we ask** or **think**, **or imagine.**"*

Her hobbies include traveling, reading and gardening.

Enrolling a child in school can be a traumatic experience for the first-time parent; especially, for the child who has experienced attachment issues, such as separation anxiety. ***Transitioning into Primary School*** is a resource that can help to decrease the stress for both the parent and child, helping the child to gain self-confidence as he or she enters the primary school for the first time or transitions from one primary school to another.

This resource book includes appropriate activities that promote ongoing interaction between the parent and child, thus providing the opportunity to build a stronger parent-child relationship. Simultaneously, the interactive exercises also present the parent with the prospect to develop dialogue with the counselor, teacher and the school and consequently encourages a healthy parental involvement in their child's education.

Transitioning into Primary School will also be a beneficial tool for the counselor or teacher to help to alleviate the difficulty of transition and make it less threatening for the child and parent. This resource book is ideal for use at any primary school on any island in The Commonwealth of The Bahamas.

>Mrs. Iris Strachan
>Counselor
>Employee Assistance Program (EAP)
>Ministry of Education

My daughter was homeschooled for pre-school. She will start grade 1 at a government school in September. After reviewing the contents of *Transitioning into Primary School,* my reservations about enrolling her in a public school with a large student population will be relieved if she can use this book.

>Ms. Ebony Brown, Parent

Transitioning into Primary School is a Bahamian book that will be beneficial to every child in primary schools throughout the Commonwealth of The Bahamas. It depicts pictures from various islands:

1. *Dean's Blue Hole,* Long Island
2. *Mount Alvernia*, Cat Island
3. *House of Assembly,* Nassau
4. *St. Stephen's Anglican Church, Andros*

This interactive resource book will undoubtedly alleviate the fears of both parent and child as the child begins primary school. Also, it will assist the counselor/teacher in making delivery of the counseling sessions lively and provocative.